SUMMONED

Toni Ortner

Goose River Press
Waldoboro, Maine

Copyright © 2012 Toni Ortner.

All rights reserved. No part of this book may be reproduced in any form without written permission from the publisher, except by a reviewer who may quote brief passages in a review to be printed in a newspaper or magazine.

Cover photo and head shot © 2012 by Janet Zimmer Photography, all rights reserved.

Library of Congress Card Number: 2012938770

ISBN: 978-1-59713-127-8

First Printing, 2012

Published by
Goose River Press
3400 Friendship Road
Waldoboro, ME 04572
e-mail: gooseriverpress@roadrunner.com
www.gooseriverpress.com

Table of Contents

Joan of Arc 1412-1431	1
Saint Teresa of Avila 1515-1582	11
Marie Curie 1867-1934	22
Rachel Carson 1907-1964	34
Mother Teresa 1910-1997	46
Elisabeth Kubler-Ross, M.D. 1926-2004	54
Bibliography	63

Preface

Summoned contains the stories of six famous women from history, each on a spiritual path. I have selected specific women who, through their positive vision, significantly altered their society. Each woman tells her story from first person point of view as I imagined it. For each of these women there was a turning point, a fork in the road, when they were summoned by a power greater than themselves to take steps that changed the conventional course of their lives and altered society. Once summoned, each woman felt there was no turning back, no matter how difficult the path. Once on the path, each woman was guided step by step. In retrospect, it all fit into place although when the women were taking each individual step, they did not perceive the ultimate goal or the far-reaching beneficial effects their actions would have upon society. Telling their stories, they reflect back to encourage and empower the women of today to have the courage to trust their instincts and intuition, the vehicle through which a higher power speaks. I, likewise, in the writing of this book, felt summoned and guided in the steps I took although I had no idea of the ultimate outcome. Whenever I attempted to do it my way, I met with resistance, conflict, and confusion. However, when I opened myself and allowed the words of these women to come through, I moved forward easily.

Traditional biographies are written in third person, present the facts of their subjects' lives, and provide a critical analysis. This book is different. While I researched traditional resources, my intuition told me to use the first person point of view. Each woman in this book speaks in her own voice and tells "her story." They come from different walks of life and are examples of what is possible. The power of these women is the power of every woman if she has the courage to follow her inner voice, instead of blindly following the dictates of society. The voices are stories of hope and possibility for the women of today. Each of these woman was an ordinary person who accomplished extraordinary things by trusting and following her inner voice. You can do the same by following your inner voice.

For the last one hundred years, American society has focused on the production of goods and on appearance rather than the quality of life and family relationships. Science and technology have been the twin gods of the modern world and the focus has been on validating evidence produced by the experimental method. The natural feminine energies of intuition, vision, empathy, and creation have been regarded as unnecessary, sentimental, and extraneous to the progress of the human race. As we enter the new millennium, these are the very energies needed to heal our society.

The book contains a bibliography of the books I read so that any woman reading the book may find information she needs to further investigate, study, and strengthen her personal awareness of these six women. Women must break free of the limiting stereotypes that have fettered them and get into action. Spiritual growth is a process, so let us begin.

I wish to thank Karen Marie Riggio for her participation in creating the first version of this book that was titled The Woman's Way but was never published.

Chapter 1

Joan of Arc

Joan of Arc (1412-1431) "Jeanne d' Arc" is a national heroine of France and a Roman Catholic saint who was burned at the stake when she was 19 years old.

***

I was born in Domremy, France during the Hundred Years War when two Popes were fighting to lead the Church. One was in Rome and the other in Avignon. There was fierce competition for land, nobility, religious power, and gold. The French had forgotten the purity of divinity. I loved my home and my family and felt pulled apart at the seam. The English military was at our doorstep. I tended sheep and goats and learned to sew and spin. I never danced with other children and loved most to go to Church.

When I was twelve at noon in the summer of 1424, I was standing in my father's garden when I heard a voice near my right hand. A great light came all about me. The moment I heard the voice, I vowed to keep my virginity. Virginity was proof of sincerity and total service in heart and body to the Lord. The voice kept coming back! It was Archangel Saint Michael! He told me Saint Catherine and Saint Margaret would come too because they were going to guide me. He said I must do the Lord's command. I must restore to the throne Charles VII, the rightful King of France. I heard St. Michael. I heard Saint Catherine. I heard Saint Margaret. I saw them! I touched them! I begged Saint Catherine and Saint Margaret to lead me to paradise, and they promised they would. They told me to remain a virgin and to continue to go to Church.

The voices told me I had four tasks. I must drive out the English. I must bring Charles VII to be crowned. I had to rescue the Duke of Orleans from the English and raise the siege of Orleans. I finally understood that the voices had been preparing me for my mission on earth. So it began.

Orleans was an important military location between the North and South of France and England. If it was captured, all of France would be under British power. I asked the saints how I could raise the siege. I was a poor peasant girl who knew nothing about riding and warfare. The saints told me to go to the city of Vaucouleurs and speak to Robert de Baudricourt who was the captain of the town. I was to ask his men to accompany me on my journey to meet the Dauphin. In May of 1428, I arranged for a relative to take me to see Lord Robert de Baudricourt. He refused to listen so I had to go back home. I felt I had failed.

The saints had showed me who Lord Robert de Baudricourt was since I did not know him. The saints promised that the third time I implored him for help, he would grant my wish. In 1429 the military situation was serious. I made a third attempt and begged Robert de Baudricourt to help me. My third appeal was granted, and he arranged for an armed escort to bring me to speak to Charles VII. The saints told me I must dress in men's clothes. I called myself "La Pucelle," the virgin or maiden and said I would remain a virgin as long as God intended. Wearing men's clothes would protect me from rape because men's clothes had many cords that tied the boots and trousers to the tunic. I had my hair cut short so I looked like a male soldier.

In February of 1429, I put on boots and trousers and a tunic and cap and left Vaucouleurs to start my mission. When I was stationed briefly in Saint Catherine de Bierbois, I wrote and sent a letter to Charles VII. I asked him to meet me in Chinon.

When I arrived in Chinon to meet Charles VII, I knew nothing of what was to happen or how I must proceed. The King was disguised as part of the crowd when I entered the castle, but the saints identified him so that I was able to speak to him. I said, "Most illustrious Lord Dauphin, I have come and am sent in the name of God to bring aid to yourself and to the kingdom. I will last a little longer than one year. Four commands have been laid by God upon me: I must drive out the English. I must bring you to be crowned. I must rescue the Duke of Orleans from the British and raise the siege of New Orleans."

St. Michael warned me that I had to tell the Dauphin about a prior experience the Dauphin had when he was alone in his garden and asked God to restore him to his throne. The Dauphin realized that no one other than God could have known his words and thoughts. Then he knew for certain that God sent me.

The King and his court were amazed by me and my

mission. I was examined physically to make sure I was a virgin. Then clerics questioned me about my religious commitments. I did not know how to respond but was told what to say by the Archangel Saint Michael, Saint Catherine, and Saint Margaret. With each test I became more determined to serve the Lord. Charles VII sent me to Poitiers for three more weeks and I was questioned by theologians. Again, I had no idea how to respond and sometimes did not understand the questions. The Saints guided me by telling me exactly what to say so that I could hold my own against these wise men.

    I was fitted with a suit of armor that fit my body perfectly and told by the saints I must carry a banner. Saint Michael described the banner that must be created. There was a picture of Our Savior holding up the world with two angels at his sides against a white background covered with gold fleurs-de-lis. It represented my people and the support of the Divine for my mission to restore Charles VII as rightful heir to the French throne.

    Protected and surrounded by soldiers, I was brought to the army at Blois, southwest of Orleans. I threw out the prostitutes from the camp. I told the soldiers they had to go to church and confess their sins; they must stop looting and harassing the civilians. When word spread that a saint led the French army, more men volunteered to join us. Finally, we left Blois and marched to Orleans.

    I carried no weapon, only my banner, into the battle. Freeing Orleans in 1428 was hard. First we attacked Saint Loup, an English held fortified church. Then May 6th we attacked a fortified monastery that controlled the Southern approach to a pair of towers called Les Tourelles located at the southern end of the Orleans' bridge. The English had been hitting Orleans with large canons from St-Jean-le-Blanc. I sent the French troops over a pontoon bridge at 9 a.m. They surprised the British and convinced them to abandon St-Jean-le-Blanc without a fight.

I led the first charge against the "Bastille des Augustins," a fortified monastery that controlled the southern approach to Les Tourelles. We were lucky and overran this with few losses.

I was warned by the saints that I would bleed above my breast during the next assault against Les Tourelles. The next morning I was first to place my ladder against the wall. An arrow pierced my chest above my left breast. It felt like a knife went into my heart. I could not breathe. My soldiers carried me and laid me down upon the ground. I pulled the arrow out of my breast and again led the rush against the wall of the fortress. The English thought I was dead so they were astonished and fell back. I still knew nothing of war and weapons but was guided to hold my banner with grace and to fear no harm.

It took us nine days and ten nights to capture Orleans. The saints told me to carry my banner high before me at all times because the French had given up hope that the Lord was with them. With the victory at Orleans, the French began to hope. Then the war with the English took a turn. The saints' voices helped me fight and win several battles. The French called me Lady Hope.

When I met Charles VII at Loches on June 11, I bowed deeply. He was so full of joy. When he told me to stand up, I thought he might kiss me. I told him that he finally had safe passage to Reims. He was coroneted on July 17, 1429, and I felt blessed to be there and share his victory. I hoped for a lasting peace, but this did not occur. There was only a short 15 day truce. Charles VII took his army on a tour of several cities to accept pledges of loyalty. What a glorious 15 days it was. When we reached Crepy-en-Valois, I hoped God would permit me to go home, but this did not happen. The short truce had given the English and Burgundians time to regroup their forces.

August 14th and 15th I led a charge against the English who held the village of Montpilloy, but after a bunch of skirmishes, both armies withdrew. My French troops went back to Crepy-en-Valois and then on to Compiegne in the northwest. The official French delegation acted as if we were losing and offered sweeping concessions to the British even though my army had advanced so quickly. This made no sense. A treaty was signed for a truce of four months. This stopped my army from continuing our offensive. We were at a standstill.

I knew in spite of the treaty, the French must control Paris. The Duke of Alencon was the only one who agreed with me. Under cover of night we moved our troops outside of Paris. A short siege began on September 8. I was wounded in the thigh by a crossbow dart. My troops fell back in spite of my urging them to attack again. On September 21 the French army was disbanded, and the French commanders were sent back to their estates. All I wanted was to return home, but instead I was moved from one residence to the next of the Royal court.

On November 4th, we had a small victory when we

Joan of Arc

captured Saint-Pierre-le-Moutier. My soldiers were in complete retreat, but I would not fall back. I shouted for the army to bring bundles to fill the town's moat. Thank goodness, I was able to start a new assault and the town fell. Our next target was the town of La-Charite-sur-Loire. The weather was chilly. My army needed food and clothes and money that we did not get from the Royal Court. We were forced to withdraw. I spent the rest of that dismal winter living at the Royal estates.

The war felt endless. Around Easter when I was in the town of Melun, the saints told me I would be taken as a prisoner before St. John's Day on June 24th but God would help. I feared treason because there was so much of it. I did not know either when or how this could happen but was told by the voices not to be afraid. It was necessary that I become a prisoner.

On May 23, when I was retreating to a town called Compiegne that I believed was pro-French, I was suddenly left alone outside a closed gate and captured by Burgundians. My worst fear had come true. I was shackled for four months as a prisoner in the chateau of Beaurevoir and then transferred into British hands. I could not understand why Charles VII made no attempt to rescue me. I was held at the fortress of Crotoy. The soldiers who guarded me threatened to rape me. I was terrified.

Pierre Cauchon, the head of the Inquisition, said I was a despicable heretic, a witch, and a false prophet. Every night I was chained to my bed. Each day hour after hour I was questioned by the clerics of the Church. I knew not what to say other than that everything I had done was done by revelation because I was told to by the Lord. If it were the will of the Lord, I would be happy to go home and be with my family. I told the men who questioned me that I neither put on men's clothing nor did anything except by the command of God and his angels.

When the clerics asked me if I heard voices, I said yes. The voices told that I would be delivered from this torture, but I did not understand how or when. The voices came each day to comfort me. Without them I would have died. I could not understand why the Dauphin did not ransom me when I was so ill and weak.

If I had been put in a Church run prison, I would be protected by nuns. I begged Pierre Cauchon to transfer me to a Church prison so I could wear a dress. He refused. I had to constantly defend myself against rape and always wore two layers of pants attached to my tunic with two dozen cords.

I was asked this question, "If the Church Militant tells you that your revelations are illusions or somewhat diabolic, would you defer to the Church?" I said, "In that case I would defer always to God whose command I have always obeyed, and I know well that what is contained in this trial comes through God's command, and what I have affirmed in this process I have done by God's command. It would be impossible for me to do the contrary, and should the Church Militant command me to do otherwise, I would not defer to any man of the world other than our Lord whose good command I have always done."

Couchon kept asking me the difference between the Church Militant on earth and the church in Heaven called the Church Triumphant. I said again and again that all I had done was under the will of the Lord and the Church Triumphant. This meant that the Lord's word ruled the word of the Pope. I was declared a heretic because I followed the voice of the Lord above that of the Pope.

I begged to go to Mass but was told it would be allowed only if I removed the men's clothes and donned a dress. I put on a dress. Then the guards increased their attempts to rape me. The guards tore off my dress. They hurled the men's clothes I had worn back into my cell. I was naked and freezing. I was forbidden to wear men's' clothes again, or I would be considered a heretic, so I argued all morning with the guards and begged them to return my dress. Finally, I had no choice left. I put on the men's clothes. Pierre Cauchon tricked me; he declared I was a heretic and had relapsed. The voices told me I must not renounce God's will to save myself.

I was transferred to Rouen and put on trial in 1431 from February 21 through the end of March. The trial was supposed to be under the rules of the Inquisition so it should have non-partisan judges. I knew as the accused, I had the right to appeal to the Pope. I asked again and again for these two things, but my request was never granted. I was condemned to death on a charge of cross-dressing.

I cried and tore out my hair when I was told I would be burned to death. I would rather be beheaded several times than have my virgin body burned. If I had been placed in a real ecclesiastical prison, this would never have happened. I protested to God, the Great Judge, about the terrible grievances done to me. I said to the Bishop, "I will burn because of you." The Bishop said, "You will burn because you are a witch."

Toni Ortner

As soon as the sentence was announced, Pierre Cauchon delivered me to the bailiff. The bailiff brought me right to the executioner in a public square in Rouen. I was surrounded by 800 armed men. I was allowed to speak. I forgave my accusers for what they did and asked them all to pray for me. I asked for one thing, that a cross be held before my eyes until the life left my body. A crucifix was brought from a nearby Church. Friar Martin Ladvenu held it up in front of me until the flames rose up. Surrounded by flames, I continued to utter the name of the Lord which was the last word I said as the spirit left my body.

***

Afterwards: In spite of the fire, Joan's heart remained totally intact and full of blood. An English soldier declared he saw a white dove fly from her towards France at the moment her spirit left her body. The executioner admitted that he was damned for having burned a holy woman.

Chapter 2

Teresa of Avila

Saint Teresa of Avila (1515-1582) is called Saint Teresa of Jesus. She was a prominent Spanish mystic, Roman Catholic saint, and a Carmelite nun. Her books <u>The Life of Teresa of Jesus</u>, <u>The Interior Castle</u>, and <u>The Way of Perfection</u> are an integral part of Spanish Renaissance literature and Christian mysticism. She founded the Carmelite order that is based on poverty.

***

My name is Teresa Sanchez de Cepeda y Ahumada. I was born on March 28, 1515, in Avila, Spain. Avila is a town of stones and saints, of burning heat and cold nights, set on a stark plateau where as far as the eye can see rocks are strewn as if they were pebbles hurled by the gods. Avila is a fortress city, a city of extremes.

I was born into a wealthy Christian family whose origins were Jewish. It was the time of the Inquisition when any deviation from the specific doctrines of the Catholic Church was scrutinized. Women could only serve as nuns, but if they spoke of the visions they saw, they were burned as heretics. The Lutherans had broken away from the basic tenets of the Church; religious wars were being fought in Spain, Italy, and France. In addition, there was conflict between the politicians and the Church as each faction sought to retain ministerial possessions and acquire additional power, authority, and land. There was also division between the noble class, the aristocracy, and the ordinary person. Although convents were springing up everywhere, decadence, materialism, and frivolousness infected these sanctuaries. Social visitors were allowed to freely come and go, and the nuns' rooms were adorned with luxuries. The foundation of the church was trembling because of the greed of men.

My mother read frequently about the lives of the saints. I desired with all my heart to be a martyr since it seemed a heroic, glorious quick entry into paradise. As a little girl, I wanted the glory of paradise more than the presence of Christ and fantasized about running away from my home to die a martyr's death in a foreign land. I convinced my brother Rodrigo to run away with me to the land of the Moors where we would be graciously beheaded. Even as a little girl, I could convince anyone to do what I wanted. I packed a bag of provisions for our journey, but we did not get very far. My uncle Don Francisco Alvarez de Cepeda galloped after us. We had just crossed the bridge of Avila and gobbled the crusts of bread I brought, when he caught up to us. Sometimes I think it was fate that brought me back to Avila that morning. Caught between land and sky, I was torn like Avila is torn between the barrenness of the earth and the splendor of heaven.

My mother was a beautiful woman who died suddenly at the age of thirty three. I had not realized how much I needed her. The house felt cold without her, and I sank quickly into deep depression feeling as if I were suffocating in a dark room without a single ray of light. I ran to the hermitage of San Segundo on the outskirts of Avila and knelt down in front of the Virgin and begged her with all my heart and soul to be a mother to me.

My mother had been strict in controlling my companions so now I was free to play with my cousins, the sons and daughters of my father's sister. At 15 I was beautiful and knew it. I loved to wear exquisite clothes. I had pretty graceful hands and dark curly hair and doused myself with perfume to further heighten my charms. I used my wit to be charming and entertaining and formed an intense emotional friendship with a girl who my mother had warned me not to associate with; we became inseparable.

Then I fell in love with a boy and felt like the living heroine in a romantic novel. My mother had read romantic novels throughout my childhood and had sworn me to secrecy because it was considered a sin to read such books. I deceived my father and connived with the servants to meet this boy. This liaison exposed my father and brothers to danger because the rule of chastity was so strong that any thoughtless word or act could totally soil a family's honor. It was common to shed blood to defend the honor of the virgins in the family. As I said before, in Avila life was lived to the extreme.

I had no idea what was to become of me. Marriage terrified me and seemed an insipid boring fate. My mother had been a dutiful wife, managed a household well, given birth numerous times, then died young, most likely of exhaustion. Her one source of consolation had been reading romance novels.

There were only two viable life choices for women at that time, to be married or to enter a convent. The frivolous period of my life ended when I was 16 because my father sent me to live as a boarder at the Convent of Our Lady of Grace. During the year and a half I lived there, I began to feel happier than I had at home. Although I remembered my childhood desire to live in a nunnery, I felt no calling to be a nun. I had to reach a decision about my future, but I felt no desire for either one of the two available choices. Without a direct calling to Christ, it would be a mockery to take the veil although of the two choices, the convent seemed the lesser of two evils. I reasoned that, at least within the convent, I would not be subject to any man's will.

While living as a boarder in the convent, in an unexpected turn of events, I developed periods of high fever and fainting so I was sent back to my father's house. Although I felt unable to bear the physical hardships and deprivations that existed in some of the convents, I realized my life as a novice at the Carmelite Convent of the Incarnation, might be integrated with some of the pleasantries and comforts of the world. I knew in my heart that I was propelled into the convent to escape marriage. The most painful encounter about becoming a nun was I had to tell my father. My love for God was not half as great as the love I felt for my father. I adored him. When I told him I intended to take the veil, I had to force myself to leave him.

For the first year at the convent I served as a postulate and was allowed to wear the white veil of the novice. It was a relief not to have so many clothes; I began to see freedom was having no choices. On October 31, 1536, my father signed the contract in the presence of a notary. The nuns agreed to give me room and board for the rest of my life; my father agreed each year to give the convent either two hundred gold duchets or 25 measures of grain. In addition, he promised to provide me with clothes and books. When the contract was signed, I was filled with joy. I found myself weeping tears of joy while doing simple tasks. I learned to unconditionally accept the circumstances of my life and my situation as a gift and did not regret giving up my former life.

It was becoming clearer and clearer to me that the material world was subject to change. Real love, however, was not of this world and not of the intellect or will. A love I was not familiar with began to descend upon me like an invisible fluttering singing bird. Although I could not see or touch it, it felt more real than any material object. Since I was in unfamiliar territory and barely understood what was happening, I felt afraid. It was at this point that I understood the mind can only go so far. I felt a joy and an absolute certainty that I could not question. I was kneeling as a supplicant before a gate, yet there was nothing I could do to push open the gate. Patience, silence, and faith were all I could muster. I chastised myself for being unworthy of this grace and ate little food, did not speak, and scourged myself with metals when I was alone in my cell because I believed that I had to suffer to be virtuous; however, when I started to have fainting fits and high fevers, my father obtained the permission of the nuns to remove me temporarily from the Convent of the Incarnation so a local healer could help me.

Toni Ortner

I was never a woman who liked to waste time and felt that I must use this time of physical pain and solitude to progress spiritually. Instead of saying my childhood prayers, I felt myself lifted into the prayer of quiet and union. Through my pain I identified with the suffering of Christ and felt removed from the secular world. On the way to the healer my uncle Don Pedro gave me *The Third Spiritual Alphabet* by Francisco de Osuna. It seemed an act of synchronicity that this was my only reading matter. It described the stages of contemplative prayer similar to my own prayer of quiet and union. A local priest came to hear my confession. Strangely enough, the priest confessed that he had been living in sin with a woman for seven years. I told him to give me the copper amulet he wore around his neck that his mistress had told him to wear and had it thrown in the river. As soon as he left the convent, he felt he woke from a terrible dream and never saw the woman again.

When my period of solitude and contemplative prayer ended, the herbalist began her cure. The pain in my heart increased and I ran a high temperature. I was afraid I would lose my mind. It occurred to me that the physical agony I was experiencing was a manifestation of my belief that only through suffering could I prove my virtue and worthiness. I lost consciousness for four days, and a priest was called to administer last rites. On the fourth day I was able to open my eyes with great effort since my eyes had already been covered with wax to prepare my body for burial. I felt as if Christ had risen me from the dead. I could only move one of the fingers of my right hand. I begged to be returned to the Convent of the Incarnation and was carried there in a sheet. I was completely paralyzed for eight months and did not leave my bed for three years when I was able to finally crawl like an infant on the floor. I wept with joy that Saint Joseph had restored my health.

My father died Christmas, 1543. Shortly thereafter a painting that I loved of the wounded Christ was brought into the convent. When I looked at the painting, I could see and feel the blood pouring from his wounds. I was overwhelmed at the physical pain he had suffered for us. From that moment on I belonged only to God.

When I prayed the prayer of quiet, my mind became emptied. My memory was lost and I felt that God was within me and I was within him. I was never a woman of moderation so the ecstasy that the prayer gave me addicted me to mental prayer. This was preferable to any human relationships. I began to doubt my right to receive such moments of ecstasy since I was an imperfect sinner. While kneeling in prayer, I heard an inner voice that was clearly not my own. The voice said, "Do not fret yourself but serve me." I was afraid that the voice I heard was the voice of the devil. The inner voices continued and directed my actions. I spoke about this to my confessor, who sometimes commanded me to ignore the voices and instead carry out his commands.

I valued obedience to the Church above all else and was terrified of being the recipient of supernatural experiences. There was danger on every side. I was terrified of malicious gossip and longed for a spiritual guide. There were a series of men I confessed to and trusted, but because my experiences frightened them they felt I was diabolically possessed and did not wish to associate with me since the Inquisition would probably declare me a heretic. I was left completely on my own. The only encouragement I received was from Francisco de Salcedo who told me to continue praying no matter what.

My health broke down. I was being mocked and doubted. The entire town of Avila was gossiping about me. I needed a place of refuge to protect me from society's judgments and criticism. I left the Convent and moved to Dona Guiomar's household. There I lived in a more hospitable environment where I was left alone to pray and meditate. I clearly saw that a personal worldly relationship would interfere with my absolute commitment to God.

It was 1559, and many women suspected of heresy were sent to burn at the stake in Valladolda. When my confessor forbade me to receive communion and took away all my books, I became seriously frightened of judgment and punishment. Father Alverez demanded specific details of my illuminations and the voices I heard, but I felt helpless to accurately transmit these spiritual revelations. The persecution against me increased, and my substitute confessor said I was possessed by the devil and must be exorcised. Since the Church is my life, those attacks by men of education who held such authority made me question myself.

I saw the living Christ in my visions and learned that I must trust what is in my heart not others' judgments, criticism, and directions. I must trust my intuition. This was my faith. As my intuition and trust in myself increased, I was startled one afternoon to see beside me a small cherub holding a golden flaming spear that he then plunged into my heart. The pain was so great and sweet I wanted nothing else but to be with

Teresa of Avila

Christ. I was consumed by an absolute longing and love for God. I must be with him at all costs. At that moment, I gave up my life as I knew it and dedicated my life to serve God. I relinquished my separateness, my individual personality. I realized that my purpose in life was to be a vehicle for God's will. Whatever he demanded of me from that moment on, in spite of my doubts and fears, I must do. I realized I did not control my life, something I had always taken great pride in. I saw that my life was in the hands of God. His will, henceforth, was my will, wherever that would lead me.

I was then directed by the voices to begin a new Carmelite Order based on the principle of poverty. I understood in spite of my wealthy background that it was necessary to completely sever the material and spiritual worlds and saw that I had been utterly mistaken in believing I could obtain a higher spiritual level while continuing to grasp the material world. Perhaps my physical torment was caused by my inability to relinquish the world of the senses. Every imaginable obstacle was thrown in my way, by the nuns, the Church, the nobility, and the politicians.

Without a source of revenue it was unheard of to establish a convent anywhere. I knew that this was a necessary act of divine faith. To accept the external world as reality would be fatal. I knew absolute positive faith would manifest itself in abundance, not poverty. True plentitude is spiritual, not material. Regardless of the fears of the aristocracy, I knew that the townspeople would support these convents.

The first convent I established was the Convent of St. Joseph's. It was a strange period in my life because I was prevented from doing what I needed and wanted most—solitude and prayer. It was clear that I must use my natural abilities and wear what I now knew to be a mask, in order to win over the politicians and the Church dignitaries. These were years of excessive and exhausting travel. I felt like a fluttering bird dressed in false and brilliant plumage. My hours of respite, solitude, and contemplation were rare. I had no choice since this was not my choice. I was following instructions from a source that would be the death of my soul to deny. It might have been easier to have married a mortal man, but there was no turning back, no giving up. My sole purpose now was His. The future spread before me like the landscape of Avila—bleak, harsh, empty, and sunlit. There were miles of desert to traverse; I did not know what was coming next.

In the little free time I had, I was drawn to pen and paper. I was compelled to write the book of my life. In it I described the process of contemplation, in which I experienced the union with Christ within myself, by opening my mind to stillness and quietness—a condition in which the soul can gradually draw closer to Him. In this state of receptivity I am a vehicle to receive; it is not my will as to when and how I will receive. All I need is quiet, courage, patience, faith, and discipline. This results in true humility, a necessary prerequisite to receiving grace.

There is no force greater than the unconditional love of the Lord which is experienced by the individual when the heart opens fully. Unconditional love means the acceptance without judgment of all living beings and the removal of the desire for personal gain; the realization that each soul on earth is unique and has been born for a specific purpose that he or she alone can fulfill. This is the turning point of each human being, as it had been for me.

To give yourself in complete surrender to your higher purpose is the meaning of your life. Although I am a devout Catholic, I understand that spiritual truth is transmitted without words and deed. Words are poor substitutes for reality. The rules and conventions, the social strictures, the religious dogma, the prohibitions are nothing in the sight of the Lord. All of it is a vain meaningless dream, an illusion that will pass away. The only thing that has existed and will continue to exist from the beginning of time and forever and ever more is the unconditional love of God for his creatures and the one divine spark within us, our ability to manifest reality from positive thought. This vision is the only reality. All human beings have this miraculous capacity, which can only be used for spiritual development.

Women reading this recognize that the obstacles and the boundaries of the material world, the patriarchal society as we know it, have no power whatsoever against the power of love. Loves knows no boundaries, admits no defeat, and is drawn to the perfection of God, of which we as children of God are part of.

Chapter 3

Marie Curie

Maria Sklodowska-Curie (1867-1934) was a Polish physicist and chemist who was famous for her research on radioactivity. She was the first person honored with two Nobel Prizes, one in physics and one in chemistry and the first female professor at the University of Paris. Her achievements were the theory of radioactivity, the techniques for isolating radioactive isotopes, and the discovery of polonium and radium. She founded the Curie Institutes in Paris and Warsaw.

***

I was born in 1867 when Poland was occupied by Russia, so we were compelled to speak Russian in the schools and no Polish history was taught. It was forbidden to speak the Polish language. The denial of Polish history and heritage was one of the most influential factors that governed my life. I was born into a family of intellectuals, as the last of five children and had three sisters and a brother. Although my father was a scientist, he was not permitted under Russian law to do the work he loved; instead, he worked as a physics and

Marie Curie

math teacher at a school where my mother was the principal. During the evenings to keep our minds open, he spoke to us about his experiments, science, mathematics, and politics. We were fortunate our father was a highly educated man who had access to books and information that he passed onto us. As a young girl I was mesmerized by the scientific apparatus in his glass enclosed bookcases; I learned later these were used in physics.

Due to changes in official rules, my mother was forced to give up her position and my father compelled to find a new job. We moved to a much smaller apartment and took in boarders to augment the family income. My mother became critically ill from tuberculosis; she and my eldest sister Zosa traveled down to the French Riviera in the hope that a warmer climate would facilitate recovery, but when they returned a year later, my mother's health was even worse. My mother was the sweet guardian of my childhood. To protect us she never hugged or kissed us, but we knew she loved us deeply. Mother finally lost her battle with tuberculosis and died. She had been the cornerstone of our family because her strong sense of duty and commitment kept us together.

Sometimes similar events cluster together; shortly after my mother died, my sisters Zosa and Bronya contracted typhoid fever from one of our boarders. Bronya recovered, but Zosa died. Because Zosa had a rich and wild imagination, she told wonderful stories that made us laugh and brought joy into our home which often was sad and heavy due to the Russian occupation as well as mother's illness and death. It was a terrible loss in a short period of time, but the losses instilled a tremendous sense of survival in me and brought our small family even closer together. My father became totally devoted to our small family network and continued with his evening readings and enlightening conversations opening our minds even further to knowledge and possibility.

I had always loved to read, so I used books to escape grief and became committed to the education of the Polish people, particularly women. Because the Russians declared that women could not attend the Universities, the only way women could become educated was by subversive gatherings, so the Floating University was created. Each night Bronya and I participated in either attending as students or giving classes in science, politics, religion, literature, mathematics and the arts. We did what we could to educate the peasants also by holding small classes and tutoring.

If we wanted to get an education, it became clear that we must leave Poland. Bronya wanted to become a medical doctor and I a teacher. We decided to go to the University of Sorbonne in Paris and made a pact to pool our resources. I would work as a governess and send a portion of my salary to Bronya in Paris; then when she completed medical school, it would be my time to go.

My first job was with a family in Warsaw, but I was not making enough money. The only way I could earn a substantial income was if I moved to the countryside which was seven hours away. When I worked as a governess, I fell deeply in love with the Kazimierz Zorawski who was the son of my employers. Although his family loved me as a governess, they felt that I was socially inferior to their son since I lacked money and would not

Marie Curie

let us marry. I swore never to love again. I saw that love must not dictate the course of my life and felt that science was a calling that would not betray me. After several years working as a governess, Bronya wrote telling me to come to Paris. I wanted to go but since my father's health was failing and my sister Hela and brother Joseph in Warsaw needed my help, it was still not the right time to start my education. I went back to Warsaw, lived with my father, and took on another position as a governess to a rich family in Warsaw. There I learned about furs, jewels, fine parties, expensive clothes, and all the finer things in life, but I was not primarily interested in these things. What did interest me deeply was my desire to educate the people of Poland because I believed education of the young would save our homeland.

I had a second encounter with Kazimierz when I bumped into him while on vacation from my job as governess. In spite of the love he felt, he did not have either the courage or strength to break with his family's judgments. That was the turning point, the last straw. I contacted Bronya and made arrangements to leave for Paris. I traveled in a box car sitting on a folding chair I brought so I could travel third class, ate my own food, and dreamed about the future.

I arrived in Paris in November, 1891, and enrolled in the University of Paris, the Sorbonne. Then I changed my name to Marie. I was referred to as the Polish student since none of the other students knew either my first or last name. I was timid and spoke rarely. My sister Bronya and her husband who were both doctors initially let me stay with them even though Bronya was pregnant. It was a comfort to come home where everyone spoke Polish. Food was always abundant, and there was music and political conversation about our homeland.

The problem was that I was not up to par with my fellow students because I had so much less background in science and math than they did, and my French was not strong enough to understand every nuance of the lectures. I rented a garret in the Latin Quarter close to the University and worked day and night to master French and learn my subjects. At times I did not eat or sleep. In 1893 I received my master's degree in physics and graduated number one in my class, and in 1894 I got a second master's degree in mathematics and graduated second in my class. I was lucky enough to receive a research position with France's Society for the Encouragement of National Industry; a requirement for the job was that I had to do experiments to study the magnetism of steel.

I explained my need of lab space to friends who introduced me to Pierre Curie, then thirty- five years old and a distinguished scientist and chief of laboratories in the School of Physics and Chemistry of the City of Paris. Immediately, I knew he was a genius. He was a gentle soft- spoken man who shared my commitment to science for the sake of knowledge and society. Like me, he had no interest in material gain. I made it clear to him that I had no intention of remaining in Paris because I was going home to Poland to teach and to help free my homeland. We bumped into one another at professional affairs, and he occasionally visited me in my garret and was impressed that I lived with bare necessities. We shared the belief that people come and go, but scientific discoveries last forever and benefit

Marie Curie

humanity.

When I returned to Poland for summer vacation, I had no intention of returning to Paris. Pierre wrote me continually and said he hoped we would remain close friends and how it would be a terrible waste of my mind not to pursue a higher degree at the Sorbonne. He wrote that it would be a wonderful thing to remain side by side the rest of our lives and share life within our humanitarian dream as well as our joint desire through research to serve humanity—as a Polish poet had said, *"to build the palace of the future."* He was overjoyed when I told him I was returning to Paris to study for my Ph.D. and he proposed marriage. However he had a long wait for my decision because I was torn between my dual commitment to care for my aging father and free Poland, versus intuitively knowing Pierre was my soul mate and that I was destined to spend my life with him.

We married July 26, 1895. As a child I was known for being stubborn and a perfectionist. Because Pierre was accustomed to Alsatian cooking, I studied cooking the way I studied chemistry. We had few material possessions since we were on such a limited budget, but I embellished our small apartment with flowers I picked during our weekly bicycle excursions to his parents' country cottage. When I was looking for a topic for my doctoral thesis, I was struck by the work of a physicist named Henri Becquerel who had discovered samples of uranium released rays that left marks on photographic plates in the dark. I decided in my doctoral thesis to investigate these mysterious rays.

As soon as I finished my research on the magnetism of steels, I gave birth to our first child, Irene. In 1897 it was unheard of to be a wife, mother, and to pursue a doctoral degree, but Pierre wanted me to receive mine since I had insisted he get his before our marriage. There was no competition between us. We determined to share our research since our goal was identical.

It must have been fate that Pierre and his brother Jacques had invented an instrument called a piezoelectric quartz electrometer because, using this machine, I was able to test various elements and mineral compounds. I hit upon an ore called pitchblende that emitted strong rays, much greater than the portion of uranium and thorium in the pitchblende should have produced. I believed there must be an unknown substance within the pitchblende. Pierre was fascinated at the idea of a new element. Although it was a hypothesis, he relinquished his own research to help further mine.

By June 1898, we had samples of this unknown element that was 300 times more active than uranium. I named the new element polonium to call attention to the Russian occupation of Poland; the first paper we wrote announced our discovery of polonium. After intensive work, we found a second substance we called radium.

Although scientists were intrigued with our discovery of polonium and radium, they needed hard proof, and we needed a pure sample of this new element in order to prove its existence. The basic problem was where to get a huge amount of pitchblende. Our old storage room was too small to continue to use as a lab. We had a small bank account and decided to use it to pay for a shipment of pitchblende waste taken from a uranium mine in Saint Joachinsthal. The only available space to work was a dirty deserted unheated building with a glass roof that had been used for dissections. It was boiling in summer because of the glass roof and freezing in winter, but in spite of the irritating gases that filled the shack; these were the happiest most beautiful years of my life. When Pierre was not teaching, we worked in complete harmony to isolate a pure sample of radium. We divided the work to support one another. I stirred the pitchblende hour after hour using primitive equipment to collect samples while Pierre conducted experiments on the radioactivity of the samples.

In 1903, I received my doctorate in Physics from the University of Paris, but it was a difficult and painful year since we were so exhausted from four years of hard work in the shed. I had gotten pregnant with my second child, and as soon as I received the doctorate, we went on vacation. In August 1903, I went into premature labor and lost the baby.

The same year we received an amazing telegram announcing that the Royal Academy in Stockholm had given the Nobel Prize in Physics for the discovery of radioactivity to Pierre, myself and Henri Becquerel. Since Pierre and I had never identified the value of our work by awards, we were not affected by this honor. We were much too exhausted to go to Sweden to accept the prize; however, all the publicity surrounding the Nobel Prize made us famous as a husband wife team.

We valued our solitude so continuous requests by journalists for interviews and the hounding of photographers, as well as the society people who demanded our social presence seemed a terrible intrusion.

In 1904 Pierre was given a position at the Sorbonne that included a small lab and stipulated that I be his

Toni Ortner

Chief Lab Assistant. This job came in the nick of time because in 1904 I gave birth to our second daughter, Eve. We were fatigued frequently and Pierre suffered from rheumatism in his legs. Our hands and fingers were always burned and swollen. I was weak and lost a great deal of weight. Neither one of us understood it was radiation exposure.

Then the worst thing that I could have imagined happened. Pierre was run over and killed by a horse driven carriage while crossing a crowded street in Paris. The second I learned of his death, my life as I knew it ended. I withdrew into silence. Without his physical presence, I felt like a shell without substance. People said that my face was impassive at the funeral, but that is because I was not there. I was not there for a long time. I was with Pierre. I would have preferred to die instead of him. I barely knew at that point which way to turn or how to find the inner strength to continue. Sometimes it feels like God asks of us something far beyond our capacity. That God took Pierre from me and I was forced to continue our work alone, was crushing. Pierre and I were one. Pierre had said it was critical that if one of us should die before the other, the one who was left must continue the work we had begun even if it felt like a body moving without a soul. We did what God intended us to do and produced two beautiful girls I must father and mother.

Pierre was and remains my soul mate. We were drawn to one another instantaneously like iron filings are drawn to a magnet, recognizing in one another the clearest and sharpest reflection of ourselves. Words are the faint approximation of the truth. They are not as solid as scientific theories in which a hypothesis can be

Marie Curie

proved through physical experiments under controlled conditions in a laboratory.

After I lost Pierre, the laboratory became my life. I could not live without it. I spent every minute in it. Each of us chooses his or her means; mine are scientific apparatus. I saw that my fate was never in my hands because it was destined that Pierre and I work as one. Indeed if it were not for the instrument he and his brother Jacques created, the piezoelectric meter, I could never have obtained the results I did and never could have imagined that there existed an unknown element.

It took great courage to get up each morning and continue without Pierre. Although I felt he was with me, I could not touch him or ask his opinion when doing experiments or making formulations. No longer could I rely on our partnership and stay in the background where I was comfortable. In the past, since it was not accepted in society for a woman to stand in the spotlight, he had been the one who gave talks to various societies and put forth our papers and ideas. It became paramount for me to continue God's work. This took tremendous courage because crowds and publicity frightened me. I had to get my personal fears and personality out of the way because I had a God given purpose that must be fulfilled. Over a period of time, I began to enjoy the exposure because I saw it as another method to educate people. I was the first woman scientist; therefore, I became a model of possibility, the possibility I had long dreamed of passing on to other women.

Long after Pierre's death I became willing to request money. In spite of my personal revulsion at presenting myself in public, I knew that without sufficient funds our work could never be continued and we would never be able to fully serve the needs of humanity. I forced myself to become a public figure.

Radium is an extremely powerful substance that can be used for good or evil, as Pierre had written in the document sent to the Nobel Prize Committee that was read as our acceptance speech. All of life is about using power for good or evil. That is why we decided not to patent the process of extracting radium but to allow it to be used freely even though taking out a patent would have made us rich. We hoped free exchange and use would guarantee its good use. For us to restrict the use of radium would not serve God's purpose. Pierre and I knew were a link in the chain of scientific discovery revealing God's will to the peoples of the world.

Great scientific discoveries might seem like miracles, but the scientist in the lab knows that the hard work of other scientists and physicists led to that moment of discovery. This is because human beings are connected. It is and was our greatest desire to be free to create and to experience the joy of continuous creation which has no limits.

My mother's untimely death made me understand that life is not in the body but in the spirit. External circumstances change continually so in order to grow in spirit one cannot let circumstance, either success or failure, riches or poverty, determine one's measure of self value. One must have ultimate faith in God to stand firm. Faith is not a quest. Each event in life happens for a reason. Faith is a joy and acceptance of what is and a daily willingness to serve. All good works with pure intention serve the larger purpose of advancing

Marie Curie

mankind.

Chapter 4

Rachel Carson

Rachel Louise Carson (1907-1964) was an American marine biologist and conservationist whose writings are credited with advancing the global environmental movement.

***

My mother, although not a devoted churchgoer, was the most religious woman I have ever known. She would not trample a single flower because she knew everything in the natural world is created by God. Human intellect cannot fully comprehend the intricate orchestration and multitudinous interrelated patterns that form the great tapestry of life, of multicolored hues and variations which place humans as one species in a network connecting the vegetable and animal kingdom with wind, water, air, and fire. Therefore to destroy anything in nature would be blasphemy. All are set in motion and balanced by a force only the heart can know and the intellect can never fathom.

The happiest years of my childhood were spent alone with mother wandering through the meadows and forests that surrounded our home. She taught me that every bird and leaf and tree was unique; each was designated by a different name and identified by specific characteristics. Her motto was to take nothing in nature for granted, to observe closely, and to record accurately. In fact, she encouraged me to keep notebooks that contained accurate detailed recordings of the flights of birds and the markings on leaves.

She insisted, above all else, that I develop my intellect and follow my curiosity by learning the techniques of research and that I never accept an outside source, no matter what the educational background or authority of the speaker, without checking and evaluating the validity of the information and having the courage and strength to reach my own conclusion. Because she believed education was power, she encouraged me to apply for scholarships. Without her dedication and devotion, without her inspiration and encouragement, I could never have walked the path that would be laid before me.

My first memories were of fields of Black-Eyed Susans, white flowers, and wild blue violets with deep green velvety leaves. The fields of wildflowers I wandered through as a child no longer exist. The earth has been bulldozed for housing developments. The stately elms that lined the streets of small towns have died. The pesticides absorbed through the leaves have decomposed into the ground and leached into the soil where the worms absorbed them. Since a single robin eats 18 worms at each feeding, many robins have died. During my lifetime even the river that ran through my hometown became polluted, filled with industrial waste. The stars can no longer be seen in the night sky which is obscured with belching black smoke from the factories. Real vision knows that man is one infinitesimal part of the balance of nature and to destroy that balance is to annihilate the human species.

In addition to my mother, there were many pivotal women in my life. Each woman appeared at a fortuitous moment when I had to make a choice that could lead me further along my path. How do any of us explain the miraculous encounters that occur in our lives when we feel in instant affinity for a stranger who without pay or ulterior motive is willing to do anything to enable us to continue walking the path?

When I was a young girl, I believed I was a writer. I longed to see the ocean so in writing created vivid images of the sea coast and ocean. Although I was a literature major in 1925 when I entered the Pennsylvania College for Women, my intellect was stimulated more and more by working in the lab of the biology department. My reasoning ability seemed suitable for the field of biology. Instead of just observing the natural world, I could understand its processes. I became absorbed in the sciences of bacteriology, physiology, and zoology and decided to major in science then get a master's degree in zoology at John Hopkins University.

Other than my mother, Mary Scott Skinker became the most important woman in my life. She taught the first biology class that I took and was passionate about preserving the natural world. She also supported me when I applied for a beginning investigator in research position to study marine biology during one summer at the Marine Biological Laboratory at Woods Hole. It was there that I first began to wander among the miraculous tide pools, and what I saw and read in the library there was the impetus for all my books about the sea.

Mary Scott Skinker understood how difficult it would be for me to earn a living in academia since I lacked a Ph.D and was not affiliated with any institution, so she set up a meeting with Elmer Higgens who was destined to play a critical role in my combined career as a writer/scientist. In 1929, at John Hopkins, there were few women who were candidates for a Master's degree in zoology. I graduated in 1932.

In 1935 Elmer Higgins needed someone to write scripts for short radio programs on marine life and gave me the opportunity to write these scripts. His offer was a turning point in my life. When the radio broadcasts were a success, he asked me to write an introduction to a government brochure on marine life, so I had finally found a way to combine my writing skills and knowledge of biology. He continued to encourage me and suggested I send articles to the Atlantic Monthly.

In 1937 family tragedy and crisis struck when my older sister Marion died at the age of 40, leaving two children. Although I was only thirty, I took on the responsibility of raising her children; Mother moved in with me as a housekeeper. It was even more critical that I earn additional money to support the family; the single means of increasing my income seemed to be to continue to write and to publish articles.

My first article "Under the Sea" appeared in the Atlantic Monthly, in which I expressed my vision of the unity of nature. The senior editor at Simon and Schuster happened to read the article, phoned me, and asked if I planned to write a book on the subject. The famous illustrator, Hendrik Villan Van Loom, set up a dinner party where I was then introduced to the president of Simon and Schuster so the outline for *Under the Sea Wind* was created.

The theme of reincarnation permeates *Under the Sea Wind.* Unfortunately, in 1941 less than one month after the publication of the book that focused on the unity of nature, Pearl Harbor was bombed so national attention, particularly in the fields of news and publications, was focused on destruction and our entry into the war. Because of this the book never received either the attention or publicity it deserved.

Once again divine intervention rescued my cause when The Bureau of Fisheries where I worked was called upon by the government to help the war effort in providing research and advice on tides. I had access to government data regarding experiments with chemicals during the war and the effect of their use on humans and the natural environment.

As my duties in the Bureau of Fisheries expanded, I began to write numerous articles, brochures, and newsletters. The majority of the articles demonstrated the effects of massive insecticide spraying on nature. I needed a deeper understanding of the interrelatedness of sea animals, climates, and tides on a global basis, so I started research in what became my second book, *The Sea Around Us.* Between the publication of my first book and the second, I lost my dearest friend and mentor, Mary Scott Skinker. I had, however, developed a friendship with Shirley Briggs who also worked for the government. Once again providence played a role because Shirley introduced me to Marie Rodell who became my literary agent. Shirley Briggs helped me to develop my scientific knowledge and skills while Marie Rodell fine tuned my writing abilities so my work became more accessible to the general public.

In August of 1950 I found what I thought were several small cysts in my left breast and went to my general practitioner for a routine physical exam. He advised me to have the cysts removed. I had a small cyst removed in 1946 from same breast, so I was not overly concerned. The surgeon I wanted to use at Doctor's Hospital in Washington was too old to perform the surgery even though he had a fine reputation, so I settled on a surgeon named Dr. Sanderson. The operation took place on April 3 and the doctors found two tumors in my left breast. Although one tumor was benign, the other was suspicious enough to require a radical mastectomy. I was in the hospital six days and in tremendous pain. The lymph nodes on the left side had been removed along with a large portion of the pectoral muscle. I asked Dr. Sanderson to tell me the results of the pathology report, and he said that I had a condition verging on malignancy. The implication was that the radical had been a precautionary act. He told me that no follow up treatment was advised.

Since I had spent most of my life being self-sufficient and caring for others, I felt any further attention to my own physical condition would be self pity and a waste of time. I implicitly trusted the words of my surgeon as so many women trust male authority figures to make medical decisions for them. By December I was in pain and regretted that I had not chosen my surgeon more carefully and had not asked for a second opinion or investigated the prognosis. The thing was I needed to be well and wanted to be well so in spite of my scientific training, intellect, and discipline, I fell victim to observer bias. I saw what I wished to see so I could continue to focus all my energy on earning a living and producing a body of work in my free time.

When I was doing research for *The Sea Around Us,* I visited Maine and sensed that was where my soul needed to be. It became clear that my purpose on earth was to write full time, but I had no idea how this could be achieved since I had to work full time to support my family. Once again divine intervention found me. Immediately after the publication of *The Sea Around Us,* I was granted a Guggenheim Fellowship, given the Book Club of the Month Award, and numerous other awards, citations and advances that enabled me to stop working for the government and write full time.

In 1951 when *The Sea Around Us* was published, I decided to control the publicity of the book and spent a great deal of time on book tours, radio shows, giving speeches, and appearing at press conferences and book parties to promote it. My vision of the unity of nature became a badge of courage I carried everywhere. Reviewers who refused to accept that a woman scientist could write as well as a man made me a target of sexist comments. When focus was directed on my gender and appearance, I refused to engage or deal with any of the sexist comments. I was determined to show that scientific knowledge was not reserved for the few but accessible to the general public who had a deep yearning for the facts and dangers of the natural world and its role in the life of every human being.

My life was lived by extremes. Extremes, I admit, are not helpful in reaching one's ultimate goal. I was afraid of being emotional, self-indulgent, or preoccupied with my body. It always felt like there were just two choices. One choice was to be independent, rigorous, disci-

Rachel Carson

plined, career oriented, self supporting and objective while the other choice was to give oneself to a man in the hopes he would take care of me.

I had observed my father's financial inadequacy and the effect his early death had on my mother. I had witnessed my sister's dream of reliance on her husband as the sole means of emotional and financial support which resulted in her despair, illness, death. No wonder I choose option one.

I admit that I might have lived longer if I had used my scientific training, my photographic memory of details, and my observational powers and focused them on myself. I should have asked for a second medical opinion from another surgeon. If this had been research I was doing on someone else, I never would have made such a grave error in judgment. I victimized myself by long grueling hours of work without sleep, pushing myself to meet deadlines and without eating decent meals. I must have felt that my womanly skills of nurturing must be directed at family members. I guess I never learned how to nurture myself.

I met my neighbor in Maine, Dorothy Freeman in July of 1953 when mother and I moved into our newly built cottage on Southport Island. With Dorothy I felt unconditional love and acceptance no matter what I was doing not as Rachel Carson, the author of *The Sea Around Us,* but as the girl, the young woman and the mature woman I had become. The relationship that I shared with Dorothy was radically different than my relationships with other women. The bond we shared was our delight in the transitory moments where together we witnessed the migration of geese along the evening skies of autumn, the sounds of the thrush at dusk in spring, or exploring the rocky shores near our homes in Maine. Even though for most of the year we lived apart, we kept in constant touch by letter and telephone. Her husband Stanley understood that the love Dorothy and I felt for one another helped each of us to become more spiritual and full of grace. The years of our friendship made me feel that at last I had come home or found what some might refer to as my other half. Because I met her toward the end of my life, it came as a special final gift because I had felt so alone.

Dorothy was my kindred soul. Because the depths of our love was unusual in our society, she was afraid some of our letters might be used to malign and disparage my reputation as a scientist; therefore, we devised a method of writing letters, in which one letter could be read aloud to family and friends, while the smaller letters we referred to as apples, contained private comments we confided in one another. This way the core of our relationship remained inviolate, intact, and protected from malicious gossip or the judgment of society. It was clear to us that other women of prominence in history who had not destroyed personal documents later became subjects of biographers who disparaged their scientific or literary achievements because they were women. I had no desire to have my personal life discredit my scientific body of work. The world I grew up in and worked in was a sexist society, and I knew that after my death my work would be judged by the papers I left behind.

As a result of the success and sales of *The Sea Around Us,* I was given a contract to produce a third book, a shoreline guide entitled *The Edge of the Sea.* It was published in 1954, and a film version of the book

Rachel Carson

was also produced. At this time, my niece Marjorie gave birth to her son, Roger. Since this was a child out of wedlock, I did everything in my power during the pregnancy to protect her privacy. Often, when I was helping her, I covered for her by telling people that I was busy with my research.

After the massive spraying of DDT on Long Island that destroyed many bird species, I was approached by an advocacy group. I began intensive research to uncover the effects of pesticides, insecticides, and other chemical products on nature, the environment, the sea, the land, as well as on human health and reproductive ability. If the eggshells of birds were becoming too thin to hatch and the reproductive rate of specific bird species was declining rapidly after the massive spraying of insecticides on plants and trees, I wondered what long range health hazards this would pose to human beings since we are all part of one system. When I began this project, I had no idea of the vast amount of information available or the extent to which I would rely on others to provide valuable information.

The Great Cranberry Scandal highlighted the inadequacies of governmental protection. Radioactive contamination of the oceans and pollution of the earth by man-made toxins seemed a great threat. The more I researched, the more I became enraged and deeply concerned for the ultimate fate of human beings. Corporate greed could not be stopped, and I felt the American public was either not informed of the facts or misled by omission.

This led me to write *Silent Spring* which I knew would be attacked violently for its content. I knew I would be attacked personally. Although I was getting weaker and weaker from the breast cancer which was spreading and the radiation to treat it, I felt, regardless of my physical pain and deterioration, called upon to complete this book. I knew the powerful chemical industry would use every possible means to discredit me and what I uncovered in *Silent Spring*. I kept my own health a secret to prevent gossip. When I appeared in public, I hid the state of my health and swore Dorothy to absolute secrecy, even instructing her to tell everyone I had eye trouble but never felt better. *Silent Spring* was published in 1962.

In the hope that I could convince the American public of my credibility and pure intention, I agreed to one TV Interview. Fortunately, President Kennedy believed in what I had uncovered and set up a Congressional Committee to investigate the effect of pesticides. The President's Advisory Committee and the Senate Operations Subcommittee made a report titled "The Uses of Pesticides." This report vindicated my evidence and concluded that the use of pesticides must be reduced and controlled. I testified before the Senate Committee and appeared on CBS national TV where I was interviewed by Eric Sevareid. While I believe I did open the eyes of the American public to the dangers and costs of misuse of pesticides, herbicides, insecticides, and other chemicals, looking back it was only a first step. Much more work needs to be done to secure accountability and uncover more chemical misuse, dangers and effects.

Already, in your lifetime the ozone hole has appeared, climate patterns have been altered by excessive carbon dioxide emissions, the oceans are becoming warmer and more acidity and more extreme weather

Rachel Carson

events seem to be occurring. Far too many animals and plant species no longer exist. Others like the polar bear, whale, and the gray wolf are among those threatened. As I and many others now see it, the final choice is either annihilation or rebirth. The result depends on how many of you are willing to turn to a light you cannot see, a light that is visible to your heart. Do not look for another source to save the world. You can no longer live in the illusion of separateness and survive. I believe that human potential is not limited, and whatever you choose to believe your potential to be can be actualized.

I was an advocate for nature because I had no choice. When I saw the results of the massive aerial spraying of insecticides and pesticides, I knew I must speak the truth. Regardless of my intelligence, discipline, research skills, or determination I could not do this work alone; I do not believe I could have walked the path I did without the divine assistance I received. Whatever changes or awareness my books brought about, they were written through me not by me, and strictly for the benefit of mankind.

Chapter 5

Mother Teresa

Mother Teresa of Calcutta (1910-1997)—now Blessed Teresa of Calcutta is regarded as a heroic Saint of the Poor; she founded the Missionaries of Charity Sisters.

***

You know me as Mother Teresa. I was born as Gonzha Agnes Bojaxhiu in Skopje which is present day Macedonia. In 1979 I was awarded the Nobel Peace Prize which I accepted in the name of the poorest of the poor, to whom I had devoted my life. I hoped that by my acceptance of the prize, the world would acknowledge the power of the poor to teach us the real meaning of humility and love.

Having a calling is not something one chooses. It has nothing to do with your personality, circumstances, needs or desires. I am not more exceptional than any woman who is reading this book; in fact, I am quite ordinary. Although I can only now recount the circumstances of my life that led me to the moment on September 10, 1946 when I was summoned, I did know then, at that moment, that there was no choice. When you take a leap of pure faith, you find yourself suddenly in a room without walls in front of a door that opens into light. There are no more dichotomies; no more black or white, no more judgments, no more boundaries, and it is clear that the intellect is but a paltry thing. When you leap into the essence which is unconditional love, you suddenly understand that the meaning of your life is to be a vehicle for unconditional love and to let it flow through you.

Unconditional love is what God feels for each of us. God makes no distinctions between the rich man and the leper, between the alcoholic and the murderer. God does not mete out judgments, limitations, nor differences. Boundaries are nonexistent in the world of the absolute. Unconditional love is the foundation of all who live and breathe. The Lord exists for each of us, only as much as each of us manifests the Lord's love so we can see that Godly love as it manifests in actions. For love to be enlivened, it needs to be actualized, to be reflected, to shine through daily choices.

I was called and I followed. The choices were shown to me, and I trusted what my heart and intuition told me to do. All women possess the same unique God-given ability to follow their hearts and intuition, to be true to what they know is their highest nature, to create a vision and by absolute faith and the certainty of that vision, to affect a change in the material world. There have been many women before me who have done this and many who will follow after me. We do not consider ourselves extraordinary. We do what God tells us we must do.

I left my home when I was 18 in 1928 to join the

Toni Ortner

Sisters of Loreto in Ireland because I longed to be a missionary. I took on the name of my patron saint Teresa of Lisieux, who died of tuberculosis at a young age. Her nickname was the Little Flower of Jesus. Although she did not grow to be an old woman like me, the Pope named her Patron of All the Missions of the World because this young woman had incredible love for missionaries and prayed continually for the priests. A flower speaks of beauty and simplicity. Its power is in the quiet radiance of its presence. A flower asks that you bask in the light of its presence. Although the life of a flower is short in terms of the span of human life, the effect of its presence and radiance is not connected to linear time.

There is no past, present, or future. These are the artificial constructs we create to describe the way in which we move through time. Separateness is an illusion. We are all a part of God, and God is within us. We are not divided by religion, race, color, or gender. The spirit is limitless and has no differences or boundaries. We are each here for only one purpose and that is to manifest our highest purpose. There is no such thing as fate or destiny. Each moment contains the possibility of infinite creation.

Some people say it was a waste of my time and effort to rescue the dying from the streets of Calcutta so that although they had lived like animals with maggots and filth, half eaten by rats, they might die in a quiet well lit place surrounded by love. One moment of unconditional love in an entire lifetime is all that is necessary for eternal salvation.

After I made my first profession of vows in May, 1931, I was assigned to the Loreto Entally community in

Mother Teresa

Calcutta and taught at St. Mary's School for Girls. On May 24, 1937, I made my final profession of vows and from that time on was known as Mother Teresa. I continued to teach at St. Mary's and in 1944 became principal of the school. I was there twenty years. My students adored me. I was content and protected within the walls of my convent.

While traveling by train to from Calcutta to Dargeeling for my annual retreat, on September 10, 1946, I distinctly heard the voice of the Lord. He called upon me upon me to venture into the slums of Calcutta to establish a religious community, The Missionaries of Charity Sisters that would be dedicated to serve the most destitute and dying.

Some of us are summoned, but not all are willing to follow the summons since it makes no rational sense to the conscious mind. When I was 18, I did not wish to leave a life of comfort and pleasure with my family to enter the convent in Ireland. I am no different from you. You must understand this. We are immersed from birth in a physical world of objects. It is all illusion, and it is difficult to give up the illusion of the safety of objects and the familiar.

I formed the Missionaries of Charity to serve Christ as he appears in the guise of the poorest of the poor, the homeless, the destitute, the paralyzed, the maimed, the lepers, the people who are labeled and despised as the outcasts of society. The poor are my teachers; the more I fill their needs and serve them by providing unconditional love, the higher I am propelled up the ladder of spiritual development. Love in action is the pathway to Christ.

I have been accused of wanting only to convert the

destitute and dying to my own faith because they fear most the very thing that I have entirely given myself to, the power and manifestation of unconditional love in no matter what shape it appears. The power of unconditional love, the human soul recognizes instinctively as a great power in the universe, the foundation of the universe, which in itself could scare anyone; therefore, if you believe in it, you may have to follow a path that is not, in worldly fashion, desirable. Rejecting my work or accusing me, keeps them away from what may have otherwise been the best decision of their life. God is love, and each of our lives has meaning to the extent that we manifest that love. There is so much hatred and prejudice in the world, so many boundaries. Love is the reality-the quiet space, the wordless place, filled with light in which the heart is humbled and opens. Everyone experiences moments of illumination, but most of us refuse to accept the possibility that moments of revelation are the true reality. To accept this fact would make the individual responsible and accountable for each choice, and whether you choose to act or not is what defines you.

Circumstances are presented to us as opportunities, as open doors we may choose to walk through. My Father's house is filled with many mansions means that the first door that opens into a room without walls leads into the next room. The castle of the interior is a place of silence, and the power of that silence strips away the material world which is illusion. By letting go of need, the soul can be truly free. The trappings of the world, the Cadillac and the jewels, are lead weights. That is why a rich man cannot easily fit through the eye of a needle. The world is so much more than the senses perceive. It is fear that creates every restriction and boundary in society.

Nothing is impossible except that which you believe is impossible. That is the gift all of you possess. The right choice at each crossroad is to follow what your heart and intuition tells you. When you leave physical form, one question matters. How will you respond to it? What have you done? What paths have you followed in the name of love?

I have done a small portion of the work that must be done. Unconditional love takes all the credit. Unconditional love is a magnet. I could never have done this work, except that I let God work through me and my small flickering light in the greater darkness drew others to me because they saw the door that would open, the door called hope, a place of light, that they, by their own actions, might enter. When this occurs to each of you, as ordinary as you believe yourself to be, you, too, will manifest divinity.

Christ felt unconditional love for the every human being. He took on their suffering as his own. That is why whenever you allow yourself to feel unconditional love for another human being, you enter into his/her feelings. If he/she feels grief, rage, guilt, or terror and you truly wish to heal them, you must first experience what they feel.

On the soul level each person understands that to feel unconditional love you must have the courage to be alone, to stand alone, to beg for help from the Lord and possibly not get it because the Lord Himself, knows that in order to be a worthy vehicle, in order to be a pure vessel, you must become the other, become thy neighbor. The results are only possible by that which you choose and are willing to do. Prayer allows God to give you the courage you need to do what is right to do. Only by becoming the other, voluntarily taking on his terror, pain, grief, and guilt can you attain the ability to remove that which causes the pain and completely heal it.

Most people avoid unconditional love because it means to open your heart to another no matter what their terror or circumstance, to be crushed as they have been crushed, to attempt to escape in the manner they did, to comprehend the many ways and means they have used out of desperation to protect themselves from encountering their deepest fears by denial, repression, alcohol, cocaine. When the numbness wears off, the individual is back at the circumstance in which he/she originally faced the terror. He/she is brought back to this point because he/she must face it head on and walk through it to let it go. If you are truly with that person in spirit, when this happens, you must walk voluntarily through the terror in order to help him/her let go. You must be clear enough to let the terror pass through you as if it were passing through purified water; this will cleanse you and the other simultaneously.

Until you have the courage to help others release their fear, stand in their place and not merely observe them, since fear is the direct opposite of love, you are not capable of being a messenger bearing love to the many. You must work upon yourself and no one else. For two persons to work together means they must work together in spirit. It is a marriage of and entirely for the spirit and is a sacred opportunity to heal oneself, the other, the many. All you need is the courage to

Mother Teresa

keep your heart open once it starts to open, to experience what the other has and still holds (the negative emotions) that have formed, the blockage that prevents the other person from loving. Face each terror that has held you back over the years. Voluntarily support each other to do this. Become a vehicle bearing unconditional love.

Chapter 6

Elisabeth Kubler-Ross, M.D.

Elisabeth Kubler-Ross, M.D. (July 8, 1926- August 24, 2004) was a Swiss-born psychiatrist, a pioneer in Near-Death studies and the author of the groundbreaking book On Death and Dying (1969) where she first discussed what is now known as the Kubler-Ross model. In this work she proposed the now famous Five Stages of Grief as a pattern of adjustment. The stages are denial, anger, bargaining, depression, and acceptance. Each person experiences these stages when facing death. She is credited with having begun the hospice movement.

***

The name of the place was Maidanek, a former concentration camp. I had come to Poland after I obtained my medical degree in order to help rebuild what had been shattered. I had always sensed that my journey would lead me into a place of ashes, silence, and stone. There was no smoke left in the chimneys. There were piles of babies' shoes, human hair, and human skin made into lamp shades. The gold filling from the prisoners' teeth had been removed. I was standing in a bar-

Elisabeth Kubler-Ross, M.D.

rack surrounded by hundreds of bunks and glanced at the wall above one of the bunks. At first glance, I thought it was a random drawing scratched on the wall. It was a butterfly. Looking around I realized that there were hundreds of butterflies scratched on the walls; at that instant I understood that nothing that happened was an isolated event. I stood in the center of an enormous silence, surrounded by thousands of butterflies. The butterflies were engraved upon my soul, inexplicable, indecipherable like a key to a door I must open. Although I had no answers and lacked basic medical equipment there, I felt hope.

I was born the frailest of the triplets, and during Holy Communion the priest gave each of us a name; mine was love. Nothing is random in the universe because from the start as a four pound weakling, I fought to survive against all odds. I loved my family deeply, but there was no way I could have stayed at home regardless of my father's determination that I become his administrative assistant in running the family business. In spite of my longing for familiarity and enjoyment in the opulence of material possessions, I wanted to go to medical school at the University of Zurich to become a physician. After graduation, I traveled to Poland to work with a relief group. I was doing construction and carpentry, sleeping on the ground, literally making meals out of air and wishing I could multiply loaves to feed the hungry. I tried to help the best I could even though I lacked equipment. The ill and wounded waited in lines outside my door. I hardly slept but was not tired because I was doing what needed to be done.

One night a woman came to me carrying her son

who was dying. I had to get him to the hospital, so the mother and I walked all night and took turns carrying him. When we reached the hospital, the doctor refused to take him because the boy's illness was contagious and the hospital beds were filled with patients dying from an epidemic of typhoid. I refused to leave until the hospital admitted the child. The doctor instructed the mother not to return to the hospital for three weeks. When I woke up in the morning three weeks later, I found by my door a small package tied with a cloth which had been laid at my door. When I opened it, I understood that the boy had lived. The mother had given me a piece of the soil from her village; she had walked all night to lay it on my doorstep. It was the greatest gift I ever received.

When I first met Manny, I knew I would marry him, but I did not see that my time with him would prove to be a brief sojourn in the singular journey I was destined to take. I followed him to New York where I worked from 1959-1962 in the psychiatric ward of Manhattan State Hospital. I worked with schizophrenics who had been labeled incurable. Because I was a simple woman in spite of my technical background and medical training, because I had confronted death in Poland when I worked with the refugees, I did not distance myself from the psychiatric patients. In my heart and soul I did not believe there was such a thing as incurable. I believed that medical training was most effective when combined with the doctor's open heart and soul. Instead of relying on Thoraziane and other psychoactive medications to keep the schizophrenics under control, I crossed the line between doctor and patient and formed a genuine relationship with each patient. I knew

Elisabeth Kubler-Ross, M.D.

that I was right in spite of the tremendous hostility from my supervisor and fellow residents. Within the two years I was there, because of my approach, so-called incurable schizophrenics left the hospital and were able to lead comparatively productive lives in society. Although the staff and my supervisors did not approve of my unorthodox choices, I knew in my heart I had chosen the right path.

I struggled to be a good wife, develop my own career, and get pregnant. I had several miscarriages before I finally gave birth to a beautiful baby boy. I struggled to balance child care with the long hospital hours, cooking, cleaning, shopping, and became even more determined not to relinquish my career. I had no idea what might be the next step of my career. Perhaps I sensed the ultimate goal although I could never have formulated it in words. I was not a woman destined to have a life-long husband, yet I never would have divorced him. He divorced me because the steps I was compelled to take in my own inner growth were alien to him, perhaps even frightened him.

I am an honest woman, so despite society's restrictions and fears, I was determined to keep a detailed record of my spiritual evolution. I was never the type to believe in meditation, reincarnation, out of the body experiences, visions, fairies or guides. Neither did I believe in babas, gurus or hallucinogenic drugs, yet my entire life I remained willing to receive and be a reliable witness of whatever I encountered. I lost my fear of death the afternoon I stood alone in the barrack of Maidanek. The butterflies were a message that I would decipher eventually.

When I worked as Assistant Professor of Psychiatry

Toni Ortner

at Billings Hospital at the University of Chicago between 1965-1970, four students at the University of Chicago Seminary asked me to provide information about the transition between life and death. I knew nothing about this subject. My teachers would have to be the patients, the terminally ill in the hospital where I worked. If there is one thing that a doctor does not want to deal with, it is a dying patient because, to a physician, death is a failure. The entire routine and structure of a hospital isolates and cordons off the dying as if death were a contagious disease when the one thing that the terminally ill patient needs is someone to listen to whom to tell the truth.

My seminars on death and dying gave the individual dying patients an opportunity to tell doctors, social workers, residents, nurses, and priests what they felt as they approached death. Since every human being needs to feel useful to the society, this gave the terminally ill patients an opportunity to speak about a taboo subject, to play an important role in the process of how professionals should deal with death, a process that would assist the patient through the process of dying and educate the professionals so that could better serve the patients.

I did not consider myself to be a writer and had not intended to write so many books. Gradually I came to understand that those who were dying went through a sequence of noticeable stages that moved from denial to anger, bargaining, depression, grief, and acceptance. If the dying are permitted the opportunity to freely express their emotions in a nonjudgmental environment, they are able to review their lives, finish unfinished business, make peace within themselves and let

Elisabeth Kubler-Ross, M.D.

go.

Death was avoided in the hospital at all cost. For example; stripping the terminally ill of clothing and putting them under glaring light far from nursing stations because they are hopeless and not allowing them to see loved ones except for a few minutes each hour, is painful to both the dying as well as his /her loved ones. Because of hospital rules and regulations, relatives are sometimes not even present at the moment of death. As a result, during the last 100 years the majority of people have grown completely out of touch with the knowledge that if one is to live fully, we must integrate and accept that death is a part of life.

I came to the conclusion that what we call death is certainly an end to our sojourn in the physical body, but it is merely a transition to another freer, far greater dimension just as the moth emerges from the cocoon and becomes something entirely different and beautiful. My work with the terminally ill reinforced my understanding that each of us has a spiritual self, an intellectual self, a physical, and an emotional self. To believe that one is only one's body is to demean and sabotage the intrinsic meaning of one's life. Each of us was chosen to be here for a specific purpose. When you find the purpose and are on your path, there is no turning back. A truly open heart is capable of miracles. What we call a miracle is an open heart that is a different higher or deeper level of consciousness. It is inevitable that when you are on your path people on similar paths will seek you out, wish to be with you and follow you.

It is such a terrible thing to witness a human being die alone in an antiseptic room of a modern hospital.

Toni Ortner

We must continue to turn things around. There must be hospices where the terminally ill can be surrounded by their loved ones and familiar objects, where they can peacefully make the transition between life and death. Compassion is like a well where the water remains pure and abundant. One drop of compassion feels like an ocean because there is so much suffering around us.

I tried to establish a beautiful farm in Virginia for children who were dying of AIDS. My farm was burnt to the ground by a hostile community; however, as a result, it enabled me to travel all over the world and give hundreds of lectures. I was led to read the books of Robert Monroe, a famous researcher in out of the body experiences and decided to visit him. I agreed to be a subject for his out of the body research and went into a modern fully equipped lab so that my experience could be documented. My conscious awareness left my body almost instantly and traveled faster than I could have imagined.

I spent that night alone in a cabin on Robert Monroe's property and it was a tortuous night. There was no telephone. No one could hear my cries for help. During that night I experienced 1000 deaths of all the patients I had helped transition from life to death. As soon as one death ended, I barely had a second to catch my breath, before the next death began. I pleaded and begged for a shoulder to lean on and heard the words, "You shall not receive." I begged for hand to hold, but I was denied that too. Even a finger would have been some comfort if it had materialized. I believed that God gives you what you can handle. Damn, if I could not even have a finger, I would not ask for it. I would get through this alone. As soon as I thought the word yes,

Elisabeth Kubler-Ross, M.D.

I accept whatever is happening, the intense physical pain stopped. Before me a white lotus flower appeared, and I was drawn into it. Behind each lotus flower was another, and I was being drawn into the heart of light, the most beautiful light I had ever seen. As it enveloped me, I felt utter tranquility and peace and fell into a deep sleep. Just before I fell asleep, I heard two strange words that I did not understand. They were Shanti Nilaya.

I awoke at sunrise and knew I should put on my robe and walk down the hill to see the sun rise. I could feel the intense vibrations of every leaf, petal and stone. I felt as if I were walking on air. At a later time I was told that Shanti Nilaya means the Final Home of Peace.

Whenever I thought that my work had ended, a new door opened. In 1977 I was led to a beautiful piece of land in Escondido, California where I established Shanti Nilaya. I began conducting week long workshops for not only the terminally ill but for anyone who worked with the terminally ill. Sometimes there were as many as 70 people in a workshop. After two days of intimate sharing in an atmosphere of unconditional love, the participants were able to resolve crucial issues. By the end of the week the participants, both the dying as well as the medical care givers, were able to experience self-acceptance, self-forgiveness, and self-love. Freed of the burden of guilt and fear, the participants were finally able to experience and transmit unconditional love.

Not everyone has understood the work I have done. I was called the Lady of Death and Dying, but the final message I was to transmit was the original message of the butterfly etched on the walls of the concentration camp. There is nothing to fear. There is no death. Give unconditional love. Find and trust your higher purpose. Open your heart today while you are still in your physical body. Be the butterfly now.

Bibliography
Joan of Arc

Permoud, Regine and Clin, Marie-Veronique. <u>Joan of Arc: Her Story:</u> Jeremy DuQuesnay, translated. New York: St. Martin's Press, 1999.

Trask Willard. compiled and translated. <u>Joan of Arc: In Her Own Words.</u> New York: Turtle Point Press, 1996.

Saint Teresa of Avila

Clissold, Stephen. <u>St.Teresa of Avila</u>. London: Sheldon Press, 1982.

Hamilton, Elizabeth. <u>The Life of Saint Teresa Of Avila</u>. Wheathampsted, Hertfordshire: Anthony Clarke Books, 1982.

Hetzfeld, Helmut A. Santa Teresa de Avila. New York: Twayne Publishers, Inc. 1969.

Petersson, Robert T. <u>The Art of Ecstasy: Teresa, Bernini, and Crashaw.</u> New York: Antheneum, 1970.

Marie Curie

Birch, Beverly. Marie Curie. Milwaukee: Gareth Stevens Publishing, 1988.

Conner, Edwina; Richard Hook. Marie Curie. New York: The Bookwright Press, 1987.

Curie, Eve; Marie Curie; Vincent Sheen translator. Madame Curie: A Biography. Garden City, New York: Doubleday, Doran and Co., 1937.

Grady, Sean M. The Importance of Marie Curie. San Diego, CA: Lucent Books, 1992.

Pflaum, Rosalynd. Grand Obsession: Marie Curie and World. New York: Doubleday, 1989.

Pflaum, Rosalynd. Marie Curie and Her Daughter Irene. Minneapolis: Lerner Publications Company, 1993.

Poynter, Margaret. Marie Curie: Discoverer of Radium. Hillside, New Jersey: Enslow Publishers, Inc., 1994.

Quinn, Susan. Marie Curie: A Life. New York: Simon and Schuster, 1995.

Steinke, Ann. E. Marie Curie and the Discovery of Radium. Hauppage, New York: Eisen, Durwood & Co. Inc., 1987.

Veglahn, Nancy; Victor Juhasz. The Mysterious Rays:

Marie Curie's World. New York: Coward, McCann & Geoghegan, Inc., 1977.

Rachel Carson

Carson, Rachel. Silent Spring.
    Boston: Houghton Mifflin Company, 1962.

Carson, Rachel. The Edge of the Sea.
    New York: Houghton Mifflin, 1955.

Carson, Rachel. The Sea Around Us.
    New York: Oxford University Press, 1950.

Carson, Rachel. The Sense of Wonder.
    New York: Harper and Row Publishers, 1956.

Carson, Rachel; Linda Lear: Lost Woods: The Discovered Writing of Rachel Carson.
    Boston: Beacon Press, 1998.

Freeman, Martha, ed. Always Rachel: The Letters of Rachel Carson and Dorothy Freeman, 1952-1964.
    Boston: Beacon Press, 1995.

Lear, Linda. Rachel Carson: The Life of the Author of Silent Spring. New York: Henry Holt and Company, Inc., 1997.

McCay, Mary A. Rachel Carson.
    New York: Twayne Publishers, 1993.

Mother Teresa

Craig, Mary. Mother Teresa. London: Hamish Hamilton Children's Books, 1983.

Greene, Carol. Mother Teresa: Friend of the Friendless. Chicago: Children's Press, 1983.

Mother Teresa; Jose Gonzalez-Balado, ed. Heart of Joy: The Transformative Power of Self-Giving. Ann Arbor: Servant Books, 1987.

Mother Teresa. In The Heart of the World. Becky, Benenate, ed. Novato: New World Library, 1997.

Mother Teresa. The Joy in Loving: A Guide to Daily Living with Mother Teresa. Chaliha, Jaya and Edward Le Joly, compilers. New York: Viking, 1996.

Mother Teresa. Words to Love by. Notre Dame, Ava Maria Press, 1983.

Muggeridge, Malcolm, ed. Teresa of Calcutta: A Pictorial Biography. New York: McGraw-Hill Book Company, 1980.

Rice, Tanya. The Life and Times of Mother Teresa. Philadelphia: Chelsea House Publishers, 1998.

Elisabeth Kubler-Ross

Kubler-Ross, Elisabeth. <u>Death: The Final Stage of Growth.</u> New York: A Touchstone Book, Simon and Schuster, 1975.

Kubler-Ross, Elisabeth. <u>Living with Death and Dying.</u> New York: A Touchstone Book, Simon and Schuster, 1981.

Kubler-Ross, Elisabeth, <u>On Death and Dying.</u> New York: A Touchstone Book, Simon and Schuster, 1969.

Kubler-Ross, <u>Elisabeth On Life After Death.</u> Berkeley: Celestial Arts, 1991.

Kubler-Ross, Elisabeth. To Live Until We Say Good-bye. New York: A Touchstone Book, Simon and Schuster, 1978.

Kubler-Ross, Elisabeth. <u>The Wheel of Life: A Memoir of Living and Dying.</u> New York: A Touchstone Book, Simon and Schuster, 1997.

Kubler-Ross, Elisabeth. <u>Working It Through: An Elisabeth Kubler-Ross Workshop on Life, Death, and Transition.</u> New York: A Touchstone Book, Simon and Schuster, 1982.

Electronic Sources

joan-of-arc.org

mariecurie.org

rachelcarson.org

motherteresa.org

ekrfoundation.org

About the Author

Toni Ortner lives in Brattleboro, Vermont where she is a member of the Write Action Board, a non profit organization that sponsors events and readings for writers in New England. She hosts the Write Action Radio Hour on the fourth Sunday of each month where she interviews writers and they read their work. The program can be streamed on line at wvew.org   Toni has had ten previous books published by fine small presses. Her website is toniortner.com. Toni Ortner has three books scheduled for publication shortly.

Summoned by Goose River Press is about six famous women who heard the call of the Divine and altered their lives to change history. These women speak in first person. It is a new way of viewing history. The book can be ordered at www.gooseriverpress.com. *Summoned* can also be obtained directly from Toni Ortner at ortnerway@aol.com. Write Book Order/Summoned in the Subject Line.

The White Page Demands Its Letters was written at the same time as *Traveling, A Perspective* and offers additional insights into loss. It can be ordered by contacting unboundCONTENT.com.

Writing With Our Blood honors 20th century women: writers, artists, survivors of war. There is a section devoted to Lyn Lifshin based on letters, a section on mothers and daughters, and women friends. The book can be ordered at www.moonpublishing.com.

NOTES

NOTES

NOTES

NOTES

www.ingramcontent.com/pod-product-compliance
Lightning Source LLC
Chambersburg PA
CBHW060341080526
44584CB00013B/869